TODAY IS A GREAT DAY

TSHEPY MKANDAWIRE

TODAY IS A GREAT DAY

TAKING DOMINION OVER YOUR DAY!

INSPIRED
PUBLISHING

Today is a Great Day
Taking dominion over your day!

First Edition, First Imprint 2025
ISBN: 978-1-0370-9893-2
Copyright © Tshepy Mkandawire

Published by: Inspired Publishing
PO Box 82058 | Southdale | 2135 Johannesburg, South Africa
Email:info@inspiredpublishing.co.za
www.inspiredpublishing.co.za

This is the day that the Lord has made;
let us rejoice and be glad in it.

Psalm 118:24

Table of Contents

ACKNOWLEDGEMENTS

Firstly, I would like to thank Jesus Christ, my Lord and Saviour, for pulling me out of the kingdom of darkness into the kingdom of light. My entire life is a testimony of His saving grace and mercy.

To my loving husband, Gift Mkandawire, thank you for always pushing me to be the greatest version of myself. You are my destiny helper, and a husband God knew I needed to birth all He has placed within me. I am eternally grateful for our marriage, and I love you with everything in me.

A big thank you to my son, Ryan Mkandawire. You are my biggest supporter and critic. Thank you for always correcting me with much respect and humility. I love you.

To my mother, Charity Molefe. You are the strongest woman I know, and I thank God that He chose you to birth me. Thank you for raising me with unconditional love despite every challenge that came your way. Ke go rata go menagane mama! (I love you very much, Mama!)

I cannot leave out my spiritual mother, Jenny Weaver. Momma, you have poured so much into me since the Lord aligned our paths. You pushed me right into my birthing position without even realising it. I believe God truly orders the steps of His beloved, and I am grateful to Him for divinely setting me up with you and the Core Group Mentorship.

Thank you to everyone who guided and assisted me in putting this piece together. Thank you to the content designers and publishers. A big thank you to my sister and editor, Devereaux Morkel, for co-labouring in this assignment with me.

There are many people I would have liked to mention individually, but that would be the entire book. I am truly grateful to everyone God has placed in my life in this season, from family, my home church, friends, teams, assistants and more especially YOU, the person reading this right now. Thank you for placing a demand for greatness on me.

I pray that as you read through this journey with me, you will be challenged to know Jesus Christ more and be the greatest version of who He intended you to be!

INTRODUCTION

Today is a Great Day is a devotional by Tshepy M,
divinely inspired by the Holy Spirit.

Every single day we wake up is a day that our good Lord
has blessed us with, and there is something worth rejoicing
in and being grateful for, no matter what season we find
ourselves in.

Today is a Great Day is an active devotional designed to
help you navigate your day through quick motivational
encouragements when you need it most. The Holy Bible is
the foundation of the book, so I advise you to not only rely
on the daily readings but to strive towards having a deeper
and more personal relationship with the Lord, Jesus Christ,

through studying the Word, praying, fasting, praising, and worshipping.

Think of motivation as water – no matter how much you water the ground, if there is no seed, there will be no fruit. The Word of God is the seed and ultimately the foundation.

Today is a Great Day is real and raw. It started with just one day of being grateful to God for the gift of life, and now, here we are... Do not underestimate the purpose of the breath in your lungs today, right now, in this very moment.

My prayer is that as you go through these readings, you will be convicted to want to know your Creator, God, more than you did yesterday, and desire to become a better version of yourself today. I pray that the words on every page will challenge you to be intentional and aspire to see growth in every area of your life.

Now, as you dig deeper, you will find that on some days the content fills the page, and on other days, it is just two lines. Enjoy every moment. There is a reason for every word in here!

Please feel free to journal whatever is in your heart as you peruse through each page... Remember to write down what the Father may be saying to you as you work through the devotional.

The Father wants to commune with you. Are you ready to take the first step to make "Today a great day"?

–1–

Today is a great day to spend time with God!

The more we spend time with God and know Him, the more we get to know ourselves.

Jesus Christ has made a way for us to fellowship with our Heavenly Father.

Let's freely run into the Father's arms today.

REFLECTION

Do you feel that you spend enough time with the Lord? What are small ways to incorporate spending more time with the Lord? (Like praying while you are driving or even worshipping the Lord throughout the day as you attend to different chores.)

Jesus answered and said to him, "If anyone loves Me, he will keep My word; and My Father will love him, and We will come to him and make Our home with him."
John 14:23 (NKJV)

God bless you and remember, JESUS LOVES YOU!

–2–

Today is a great day to step out!

Some things will NEVER happen FOR you until you take the first step!

Today, be prepared to take the step that you've been putting off.

I challenge you to push beyond your excuses and level of comfort.

CHALLENGE

What have you been putting off? How can you take that first step today?

God bless you and remember, JESUS LOVES YOU!

–3–

Today is a great day to serve!

God will meet you at your place of serving.

Remember this: You serve God through the people He has placed in your path.

Never become arrogant in your serving; humble yourself before the Lord and He will exalt you (**James 4:10**). This applies to all leaders in your life – your pastor, employer, parent, teacher, husband, etc.

Each of you should use whatever gift you have received to serve others, as faithful stewards of God's grace in its various forms.
1 Peter 4:10 (NIV)

God bless you and remember, JESUS LOVES YOU!

—4—

Today is a great day for restoration!

God will restore so much in your life that you'll even forget the pain from your past!

I pray that you experience supernatural restoration for all that you have lost in the past. May you experience a fresh start even on this day!

"But may the God of all grace, who called us to His eternal glory by Christ Jesus, after you have suffered a

while, perfect, establish, strengthen,
and settle you."
1 Peter 5:10 (NKJV)

God bless you and remember, JESUS LOVES YOU!

–5–

Today is a great day to press on!

The temptation to quit every time things get tough is always stronger than the courage to pursue and finish.

We get to a point where we even question the work we have put in, whereas the seed has already started germinating.

No matter how difficult it may get, press on; you have come too far to throw in the towel.

"Let us not become weary in doing good, for at the
proper time we will reap a harvest if we do
not give up."
Galatians 6:9 (NLT)

Tomorrow you will look back and see the impact you've
made today.

You cannot get to the promise without the pruning
process. Let's go!

God bless you and remember, JESUS LOVES YOU!

–6–

Today is a great day to keep going!

While you are waiting for harvest season, don't stop cultivating other avenues.

Don't stop planting! Don't stop watering! Keep going, and soon you will appreciate your consistency.

No season lasts forever; remember that God is faithful in every season!

God bless you and remember, JESUS LOVES YOU!

–7–

Today is a great day to walk in power!

The power of a lion is measured by its ROAR. If you don't know your power, you might find yourself altering that which makes you POWERFUL!

Being powerful is a gift! Treasure it! Embrace it! Utilise it!

Remember that we are all uniquely powerful because God has made us in His very image. There's no need to be intimidated by another roar!

You are designed to fulfil a specific purpose that ONLY YOU can fulfil.

I pray that today you will discover what you were designed to do or at least take one step closer!

God bless you and remember, JESUS LOVES YOU!

–8–

Today is a great day to build!

Every day you are building and planting towards something!

You are building not just in works but in words too. What are you saying to yourself about yourself? What are you saying about your children, spouse, and marriage? What are you saying about your job or businesses? What are you building today?

Today, I challenge you to change what you say so that you can start to see the future you want come to fruition.

I challenge you to speak life, no matter what you see now!

"Death and life are in the power of the tongue."
Proverbs 18:21a (NKJV)

God bless you and remember, JESUS LOVES YOU!

–9–

Today is a great day to be intentional!

If we are not intentional about what we want, what we don't want will automatically rule!

Today is a great day to steer yourself towards the desires that God has placed in your heart. I'm talking about specific dreams and goals that you know for a fact God has placed in your heart.

Do not get distracted! Even in times of uncertainty, stay FOCUSED!

FOCUS

What are some God-given dreams that the Lord placed in your heart, which you may have forgotten or started but not finished? How can you get back on track?

God bless you and remember, JESUS LOVES YOU!

–10–

Today is a great day to trust God's plan!

Where you are now is not all there is to your life!

You need to understand that each chapter and season contributes to where you are headed! Personally, I am learning daily that there are no better plans than God's plans. There are so many times when I plotted my way out of or into situations, and God has gone ahead of me in His ways, which turned out to be far better than what I had planned.

As cliche as this sounds, but genuinely from a place of knowing, I say: "Be still in the Lord's promises for your life, and trust God always – in every season!"

"For My thoughts are not your thoughts, nor are your ways My ways," says the LORD. "For as the heavens are higher than the earth, so are My ways higher than your ways, And My thoughts
than your thoughts."
Isaiah 55:8-9 (NKJV)

God bless you and remember, JESUS LOVES YOU!

–11–

Today is a great day to examine your input!

If we want to experience a different output, we need to examine and evaluate our input.

This literally goes for EVERYTHING! From our health, work ethic, to how we raise our children, and everything in between!

Quick example: I had a conversation with my husband one day, and we spoke about how most of us had "fear" instilled in us by our parents – innocently so. You find some parents saying, "You need to do this, or else…" –

and if we pass this on to the next generation, the cycle remains the same. So, if we want to see and raise a different generation, we need to do things differently so that we may deliver different results.

The above is an example, and I hope it brings clarity and the context I'm trying to illustrate.

Today, let's examine the results we have right in front of us and trace back the seeds we've sown. If we are not happy, let's take a step to change!

I challenge you to take a step today that your future self would be grateful for!

God bless you and remember, JESUS LOVES YOU!

–12–

Today is a great day to break through!

Something has to break!

Someone must pay the price to obtain the prize. Are you willing to do what it takes?

We are living in times where we are always faced with an opportunity to move past what we have always been exposed to. May we never find ourselves settling because we refused to put in a little more effort, time, or make the necessary sacrifices. May we be the ones who set new bars, new levels and tap into the fullness of what and who God has called us to be.

As the saying goes, "It's not easy but it's worth it." Are you willing to pay the price for the ultimate prize?

God bless you and remember, JESUS LOVES YOU!

–13–

Today is a great day to discern your season!

"To everything *there is a season*, a time for every purpose under heaven."
Ecclesiastes 3:1

We need to understand and discern the seasons in our lives. There are different times and seasons in nature. Why would our lives be different? Each season serves a purpose and has its own requirements; for example, there's time for cultivating, planting, watering, waiting, and harvesting.

I'm no expert when it comes to farming; however, what I can say is we cannot cultivate in a season of watering and vice versa. This applies to our lives as well! If we are not aware of what season we are in, we might find ourselves harvesting unripe produce, which will ultimately never ripen to its full potential.

I pray for wisdom to discern what season you are currently in, and more importantly, how to safely navigate it!

God bless you and remember, JESUS LOVES YOU!

–14–

Today is a great day to push forward!

Every single day and time you are faced with a challenging situation; you choose to either push forward or back down, but there is no in between!

I challenge you to push forward today!

"'For I know the plans and thoughts that I have for you,' says the Lord, 'plans for peace and well-being

and not for disaster, to give you a future and a
hope'."
Jeremiah 29:11 (AMP)

God bless you and remember, JESUS LOVES YOU!

–15–

Today is a great day to start!

You don't always have to wait for everything to be perfect so you can start, but you have to start, so take that leap of faith!

Some things only begin to unfold when we take the first step, and unfortunately, we will never know what's on the other side until we begin to exercise our faith.

I pray for boldness over you today, that you push past and beyond any fear that's been hindering you from moving forward.

God bless you and remember, JESUS LOVES YOU!

–16–

Today is a great day to reign!

When we compare ourselves to others, we literally
abandon a banquet laid out especially for us by the Lord.
We choose to scavenge from someone else's leftovers!

We are all designed to serve a specific, unique purpose!
Imagine if the lungs tried to fulfil the heart's purpose…
Disaster! Danger!

Comparison is a complete setup for failure!

May we remember today that we all have a specific purpose to fulfil.

No one can do what you do, and you do it best as you! Reign gracefully in your God-given purpose.

God bless you and remember, JESUS LOVES YOU!

–17–

Today is a great day to be grateful!

One day, it will all start to add up. It will start clearing up; why some things never worked, why some relationships ended with no sensible explanation, why certain opportunities ceased bearing fruit, etc.

For now, it may not make much sense, and at times it may even be hurting as you ponder many questions, but allow me to tell you this: IT WILL START ADDING UP! And you will begin to be grateful as you realise that some things that seemed not to be going your way were, in fact, working out for your good.

I pray for strength and endurance as you drift through different seasons. I also pray for comfort in any area of loss. May you experience true, unspeakable joy no matter where you find yourself today!

"Weeping may endure for a night, but joy *comes* in the morning."
Psalm 30:5b (NKJV)

God bless you and remember, JESUS LOVES YOU!

–18–

Today is a great day to be inspired by YOU!

What if I told you that the very same people that you wish to be like may also wish to be like you?

Will that push you to live your life as genuinely as God would have intended?

What am I getting at? There's absolutely nothing wrong with being inspired by other people, but there is something wrong when we want to abandon our mandate and purpose in life in pursuit of trying to be like others.

Listen! We can all learn and draw from each other; every one of us has a unique blueprint.

No one can do what you do the way you do it! God has wired us all uniquely. Yes, it may seem like we are all doing the same thing, but there's a finer detail that distinguishes us all from one another. Just like you can find people who look alike, but you will never find two people with the same fingerprints .

Today, I want to challenge you to focus on what makes you unique and look for ways to serve others with that.

Be inspired by your own uniqueness.

You add value! You are powerful because we all have the identity of God in us. We were all created in the image of God Himself!

God bless you and remember, JESUS LOVES YOU!

–19–

Today is a great day to serve with your gift!

I have often heard people say that "your gift will make room for you".

I agree with that, and that is why we should stay humble and keep serving!

Remember, it's a GIFT! You did not earn it; God placed it in you, so why boast as though you earned it?

Today, I want to challenge you to look for an opportunity to serve with your gift.

"Your talent is God's gift to you. What you do with it is your gift back to God." American author, Leo Buscaglia.

God bless you and remember, JESUS LOVES YOU!

–20–

Today is a great day to grow!

Don't be surprised when certain things that used to excite you are no longer appealing to you.

It's part of your growth, and I believe that as you begin to spend time with the Lord, He will begin to put fresh desires, dreams, passion, hunger, zeal, and goals within you.

Don't be alarmed when the crowd around you begins to disperse. Some seasons will require us to outgrow some people, and that's okay!

Don't beat yourself up; instead, submit to what God is doing in this season and within your life.

Ask the Holy Spirit to grant you the wisdom to guard your heart as you navigate different seasons of growth.

FOCUS

Holy Spirit, I understand that out of my heart flows all issues of life according to Proverbs 4:23, therefore I ask that You to help me to guard my heart from offense as I navigate different stages of growth. In Jesus' Name. Amen.

God bless you and remember, JESUS LOVES YOU!

–21–

Today is a great day to press forward!

Sometimes all we need to do is to reflect on how far we've come, and that can be enough to keep us pressing forward. Your own progress can be the best motivation to keep going. You may not be where you want to be, but it is inspiring to see that you are not where you began.

Today I want to challenge you to take stock of your progress. You will begin to enter a place of gratitude and realise there is so much more to be grateful for.

God bless you and remember, JESUS LOVES YOU!

–22–

Today is a great day to do something fulfilling!

I pray that these daily motivations push and stir you towards the direction of living your God-given purpose! At the end of it all, we are still here in this world, and I believe there is a reason. I believe God has kept us for such a time as this!

Many went to bed last night with the hope of waking up this morning, but they did not! It's simply God's grace that you are up, healthy, sheltered, fed, and reading this very message today!

I pray that today you will step out and do something that will bring you fulfilment!

May you have a blessed and beautiful day!

"Yet who knows whether you have come to the kingdom for such a time as this?"
Esther 4:14b (NKJV)

God bless you and remember, JESUS LOVES YOU!

–23–

Today is a great day to run your race!

When you think you have given your all, there's still so much you can give. God the Father, Son and Holy Spirit created us in Their image and likeness; the very Triune created this earth we live in today, and God continues to work miracles!

Our God never runs out, and if we are created in His image and likeness, it means we too will never run out.

There's so much that God wants to pour out through us; however, we must be in a position to receive and run the race set before us with endurance!

"Therefore we also, since we are surrounded by so great a cloud of witnesses, let us lay aside every weight, and the sin which so easily ensnares us, and let us run with endurance the race that is set before us, looking unto Jesus the author and finisher of our faith, who for the joy that was set before Him endured the cross, despising the shame, and has sat down at the right hand of the throne of God," - **Hebrews 12:1-2 (NKJV)**

There is a reward for the completion of the race. Christ, after completing the race, sat down at the right hand of God!

God bless you and remember, JESUS LOVES YOU!

–24–

Today is a great day to focus on your journey!

We all have different races to run!

What works for you may not work for me and vice versa!
While you are using someone else's route as a GPS, you are
detouring from your path and hindering your progress!

Draw inspiration, but never get derailed or distracted.

Your path is already paved, and it shall remain uncharted
until you embark on your journey.

Like the Lord said to Jeremiah, "Before I shaped you in the womb, I knew all about you. Before you saw the light of day, I had holy plans for you..."
Jeremiah 1:5a (AMP)

God bless you and remember, JESUS LOVES YOU!

–25–

Today is a great day to be revived!

What man puts to death, God can revive! It is not over until God says so!

People may think that they have buried you either with their words or deeds, but God is able and faithful!

Some situations may have you feeling as if you are drowning in distress, BUT do not despair!

I've got some news for you: "Weeping may endure in the night, but JOY comes in the morning." I know you might have heard this before, and it may be difficult to believe now, but I declare that YOUR morning is NOW!

"Rejoice in the Lord always. I will say it again: Rejoice!"
Philippians 4:4 (NIV)

The joy of the Lord is your strength!

God bless you and remember, JESUS LOVES YOU!

–26–

Today is a great day to say YES to God!

God is not limited by time, your new year can even start right now, TODAY!!!

God has already provided what you need for the task at hand. He's just waiting for your YES!

I pray that we never miss what the Lord is doing in this season.

Today, give God your fresh YES. Have you fully surrendered to the Lord? It is never too late.

PRAY

"Lord. I repent for any time I said no. I do not want to be disobedient to You. I fully surrender to You and give You my fresh yes. Lord, have Your way. Show me the way I should go, and what I should do in this season. I do not want to miss what You are doing, Father. In Jesus' name I pray, Amen."

God bless you and remember, JESUS LOVES YOU!

-27-

Today is a great day to reignite that fire!

Some things will never move until you move!

So often we wait for people to action what's assigned to us, where the vision was imbedded specifically in our core.

No wonder we sometimes find ourselves disappointed and discouraged by what once stirred a fire in our bellies and then eventually gave it all up!

Today, I challenge you to go back to the time when God gave you that vision and take heed of every detail in the instruction! You will be surprised by how much you can achieve if you focus on the specific details and just start moving!

God bless you and remember, JESUS LOVES YOU!

–28–

Today is a great day to inspire!

Don't be intimidated when others imitate you!

Isn't it funny how we sometimes don't want to be "copied"? I used to be like that, and I would get so annoyed when others copied how I did certain things. I felt like they were trying to be me – how silly and self-centred is that? Now, I have learnt that people usually imitate what inspires them.

Let the inspiration flow.
Stop being too full of yourself.
Focus on your race.

Instead of being intimidated, aspire to inspire more!

God bless you and remember, JESUS LOVES YOU!

–29–

Today is a great day to stand out!

Do you remember the times when you used to be so scared to be different? Well, maybe you've never had that struggle, but I remember being too scared to stand out. I remember how I always wanted to fit in so much so that I would dismiss the very things that were meant to set me apart.

One day I was drawn to these scriptures:

"But you are a chosen race, a royal priesthood, a consecrated nation, a [special] people for God's own possession, so that you may proclaim the excellencies

[the wonderful deeds and virtues and perfections] of
Him who called you out of darkness into His
marvellous light."
1 Peter 2:9 (AMP)

"Let your light shine before men in such a way that
they may see your good deeds and moral excellence,
and [recognise and honour and] glorify your Father
who is in heaven."
Matthew 5:16 (AMP)

Whatever you do today, remember to let your light shine.
Choose to stand out. When we allow our light to shine, we
glorify God the Father – our Creator! You were not made
to hide but to SHINE!

God bless you and remember, JESUS LOVES YOU!

–30–

Today is a great day to remain in gratitude!

Today is a brand-new day that you will never get to live again!

I hope and trust that you will choose to be grateful for it, no matter what you may be facing right now. For those of you who may have experienced some form of loss, I pray for complete restoration and healing!

Today, I want to challenge you to take stock of things to be thankful for. Take a moment today to reflect on the good that has come out of your life thus far and shout out with praise unto the Lord!

Gratitude is a weapon that breeds more to be grateful for. The more we remain in gratitude, the more we get to be grateful!

Personally, I am grateful for you, yes you, the one reading this right now. I am grateful for the opportunity to make an impact. I am grateful that I am still alive today. I'm grateful for God's protection over me, my family, businesses, ministry, and all God has blessed me with. After all, there's so much to be grateful for even during uncertainties!

What are you grateful for today??

God bless you and remember, JESUS LOVES YOU!

–31–

Today is a great day to take control of your thoughts!

Our thoughts are like seeds. Our brains are like soil. Whatever we entertain germinates.

The Bible teaches us to take our thoughts captive, which means to arrest any thoughts that pop up, which may eventually lead us astray.

Are you intentional about your thoughts, or do you entertain whatever pops up? How do you take control of your thoughts?

Personally, when I get thoughts that I'm not in agreement with, I vocalise the opposite. My first assertion is, "The devil is a liar…" I then start to speak words that are contrary to those thoughts. Sometimes, I put on some praise and worship music and sing along or listen to an audio Bible. After all, our words have power! Death and life are in the power of the tongue, as the word of God says in **Proverbs 18:21.**

Today, let us be intentional.

Let us not allow the devil to turn our minds into his playfield!

Let us overcome by speaking life and life alone!

God bless you and remember, JESUS LOVES YOU!

–32–

Today is a great day to learn and step forward!

Every second, every minute, every hour, every day, every week is an opportunity for us to take a step towards where God has called us to, an opportunity for us to learn and be corrected!

Know this:

God has already gone before you.
What is impossible with man, is possible with God.
Greater is He that is in you than he that is in the world.
You were created for such a time as this.
You can love and forgive no matter how hard it is because Jesus Christ has done so for you.

May the joy of the Lord be your true strength on this day.

God bless you and remember, JESUS LOVES YOU!

–33–

Today is a great day to submit!

Just when you think you have arrived or reached your peak, there's more ahead. Your ceiling today may be your floor in a year's time.

God's ways never end; we are to remain in a place of submission so that we move and operate in His seasonal timing.

Personally, I'm learning this daily. I'm learning to trust and submit to God's will for my life, and I see Him transitioning me from one comfort zone to another. I am learning that nothing grows inside my comfort zone.

Today, I want to challenge you to be in a place of submission.

Ask God what He requires of you in this season and genuinely be prepared to move as He speaks. God the Holy Spirit wants to flow freely through us. As we allow Him to flow, we too are hydrated and refreshed.

Are you prepared to submit and walk in obedience today?

God bless you and remember, JESUS LOVES YOU!

–34–

Today is a great day to walk in authority!

The moment you realise that God has already validated you, you will stop seeking validation elsewhere. You will begin to walk in the authority that has been granted to you.

Imagine a lion seeking permission from a zebra or impala, or any other animal to roam around the wild. It doesn't even make a little sense. A lion knows its authority, and that's why it is a threat to other animals in the wild.

When you know and walk in your authority, you can appear intimidating.

Do not retreat! Keep at it!

You will find that when you begin to tap into who you were created to be, others will be encouraged to step into their Godly purpose too!

God bless you and remember, JESUS LOVES YOU!

–35–

Today is a great day to be a peacemaker!

Not everyone has your best interests at heart. A hard truth, but a truth, nonetheless.

In this journey of life, you will find people who made it their purpose and assignment to destroy and discredit you, BUT be of good cheer.

Have you ever heard the statement, "Hurt people, hurt people"? I've both heard and witnessed it!
When this happens, how are we supposed to respond?
Let's see what the Word of God says:

"Blessed [spiritually calm with life-joy in God's favour] are the makers and maintainers of peace, for they will [express His character and] be called the sons of God."
Matthew 5:9 (AMP)

Our response should always be aimed at peace-making – especially when it's the most difficult thing to do.

I pray that today you release and forgive all those who hurt, betrayed, and persecuted you!

ACTION

Make a list of all the people you need to forgive and choose to forgive them. Not for them, but for you.

God bless you and remember, JESUS LOVES YOU!

–36–

Today is a great day to be resilient!

Don't pack up until your task is complete!

Often as a season comes to an end or a task does not go as planned, most people close shop. Do not fall into that temptation if it was not your plan – stay focused and work on your schedule.

It is important that we understand the seasons that we are currently in. It is vital for us to understand that God's timing is not based on our schedule.

May you endure until the very end! May you endure until you are done!

God bless you and remember, JESUS LOVES YOU!

–37–

Today is a great day to see past the clouds!

This is the day and week that the Lord has made! Let us rejoice and be glad in it!

Just because you don't see any clouds today, it does not mean rain will never fall.

Do not allow your current season to hinder you from looking forward to AND preparing for your next season!

Listen, we all know that each season has its own requirements. Some seasons can leave you feeling as if you have reached the end but I'm here to remind you that as long as you are alive to even witness this season, God still has more prepared for you.

Do not despair!

God bless you and remember, JESUS LOVES YOU!

–38–

Today is a great day to focus!

Distractions will come, but you do not have to be distracted.

The word "distracted" means unable to concentrate because one is preoccupied by something worrying or unpleasant.

These days we must be intentional about pressing on until the end. It is okay to pause and regroup, but do not abort the mission because of a distraction.

Distractions are meant to deviate your attention. Distractions can instill fear, and fear can cripple you if you are not mindful.

Today, I want to challenge you to focus beyond obstacles and distractions.

Maintain your focus.

Know that God is with you no matter what, and HE WILL SEE YOU THROUGH TO THE FINISH LINE!

God bless you and remember, JESUS LOVES YOU!

–39–

Today is a great day to be thankful!

The Bible speaks a lot about being thankful. Personally, I fully believe in being grateful and thankful – always. It keeps me in a place of humility.

The more I give thanks to our gracious God, the more I realise that all I am and all I have is because of His grace!

Let's have a look at this portion of scripture:

"In every situation [no matter what the circumstances], be thankful and continually give thanks to God; for this is the

will of God for you in Christ Jesus."
1 Thessalonians 5:18 (AMP)

What are you thankful for today?

God bless you and remember, JESUS LOVES YOU!

–40–

Today is a great day to embrace God's grace!

God will grant you the grace to handle everything that comes with the life He called you to.

So many times we want to figure it all out before we take the first step. Faith is taking the first step without seeing the second one.

When God places a call on your life, He places a grace on it, too. It doesn't mean that it gets easier, but we are strengthened and comforted in knowing that God is with us every step of the way!

Rest in His grace today! It is well!

God bless you and remember, JESUS LOVES YOU!

–41–

Today is a great day to go beyond your comfort zone!

Sometimes we need to be willing to go beyond our comfort zones for us to rise to our optimal zone.

I believe that God has a specific plan and purpose for us all to attain in life, so much more than just our day-to-day activities. God placed us on the earth for His glory and to make an impact on each other's lives.

We have to be willing to die to self so we may live a life of true servanthood. We rise in our serving, and the Lord honours a servant's heart.

What are you willing to sacrifice today for a better tomorrow?

God bless you and remember, JESUS LOVES YOU!

–42–

Today is a great day for servanthood!

Serving has been so strong in my heart this season.

If we can master the art of serving and laying down any pride or the need for recognition, only then can we begin to flourish and experience God's favour in a miraculous way.

I can mention so many people in the Bible and walking the earth today who are true examples of servanthood. These people include our Lord and Saviour, Jesus!

Serving goes as deep as laying down your desires for a cause greater than yourself.

Today, I pray that you would look for an opportunity to serve and do good, genuinely from your heart, without any expectation.

God bless you and remember, JESUS LOVES YOU!

–43–

Today is a great day to be present in the moment!

Sometimes we wonder why certain things never materialise when we want them to at our desired times... Or am I the only one?

Well, I have come to realise that God's way and timing are far above our own. Daily, I am learning to live in this truth that not a single day comes as a surprise to God and each day is filled with purpose.

When we begin to live this truth, we will start to be fully present in each moment with stillness.

I pray that today you walk knowing that God has everything under His control and for your good!

"And we know [with great confidence] that God [who is deeply concerned about us] causes all things to work together [as a plan] for good for those who love God, to those who are called according to His plan and purpose."
Romans 8:28 (AMP)

God bless you and remember, JESUS LOVES YOU!

–44–

Today is a great day to trust God!

God's choices for you are way better than your own – even when you don't understand them at the time, TRUST HIM!

I'm learning this daily, and I've come to experience a peace like no other.

I pray that you learn to fully lean on the Lord. May you experience a peace that surpasses all understanding, even in this season!

"Trust in the Lord with all your heart and lean not on your own understanding; in all your ways submit to him, and he will make your paths straight."
Proverbs 3:5-6

God bless you and remember, JESUS LOVES YOU!

–45–

Today is a great day to celebrate life!

As the days go by, I realise more and more how blessed we all are just to see another day, month, and year.

Yes, it may have been a challenging day, month, year or even decade, but we are still standing by the grace of God. We get to witness another sunrise, and I declare that we will live to see the goodness of the Lord in the land of the living, as per **Psalm 27:13**.

Listen, God can turn any situation around. Many others and I are living testimonies of that.

I want to challenge you to borrow some of my faith today, especially if you feel you can't anymore. If God is doing it for someone you know, trust me, He can do it for you too.

Be encouraged today.

God bless you and remember, JESUS LOVES YOU!

–46–

Today is a great day to please the One who leads us!

Today, I pray that the Lord sets you free from the people-pleasing syndrome.

I remember at one point I used to be so concerned about what people thought or said about me until I had the revelation that I'll never live a life fully pleasing to the Lord if I want to please people.

I used to think not caring about what people think meant I was arrogant or inconsiderate – that's not TRUE!

Sometimes, we may miss destiny-defining moments while trying to please everyone instead of the One who leads us.

I am not promoting any rude or insensitive behaviour; however, I am saying let us be sensitive to the leadership of the Holy Spirit and learn to march to His beat, even when it doesn't flow with the rhythm of the world or it feels strange to our own flesh.

God bless you and remember, JESUS LOVES YOU!

–47–

Today is a great day to hear what God is personally saying to us!

What may appear unplanned to us could sometimes be ordained by God.

In our planning, let us remember to say, "Let Your perfect will in my life be done Lord."

So many times, we shut God out of "our plans" and expect Him to bless what He has not ordained.

I'm reminded of the story in the Bible when God promised Abraham and Sarah a child in their old age. It was impossible to man, but with God, all things are possible. In their waiting, they tried to fast-track God's promise and expected God to bless Ishmael, which was their plan and not God's perfect will. God's will had to be done, and therefore, Isaac was born the way God intended for it to happen.

In this season, let's learn to hear and see what God is personally saying to us.

Let's walk in obedience and allow the fruit of the Spirit to be cultivated in the process.

Remember, God has already gone before us!

God bless you and remember, JESUS LOVES YOU!

–48–

Today is a great day to be a student!

Every day can be a good day to learn something new. No matter where we are in life, there's always something we can learn from one another. I believe God is always moving, and He is using yielded vessels to equip us. If we think too highly of ourselves, we may miss the lessons that are meant to advance us.

Today, I pray that you intentionally look for opportunities to learn something new and have the wisdom to apply what you've learnt!

God bless you and remember, JESUS LOVES YOU!

–49–

Today is a great day to identify your gifts!

Every one of us has a special gift inside us.

There's something only you can do that no one else can do, and if they can do it, no one can do it the way you do it.

There are certain things that make you unique and different that other people will never understand.

Identify those things and find a way to serve and even look for earning potential through them.

You may feel as if there's absolutely nothing that you are gifted in… but let me ask you this, what is that one thing that you can do easily with minimum to zero effort, yet other people may struggle to do even with maximum effort?

For me, one of those things is speaking. For you, it may be cooking, writing, singing, poetry, administration, praying, serving, designing, teaching, creating, whatever it is – you know what it is!

I pray that today you discover your gift and make an effort to sharpen it!

God bless you and remember, JESUS LOVES YOU!

–50–

Today is a great day to forgive!

Our hearts should be like rivers and not dams. So many of us harbour unforgiveness and hold on to offence and it costs the life-flow within us.

A river flows, and there's constant life in the river.

The Bible tells us in **Proverbs 4:23** to guard our hearts, for out of them FLOWS the issues of life.

If we don't guard our hearts and permit unforgiveness, bitterness, and offence to reside in us, we will never experience and enjoy the fruits of the FLOW!

I challenge you to release all that's hindering the flow of life today and ask God to give you the strength to confront it!

God bless you and remember, JESUS LOVES YOU!

–51–

Today is a great day to create new habits!

You cannot expect new results if you do not implement new habits. It is always difficult for the mind to adjust to new things, and often, we find ourselves in a battlefield whenever we have to divorce the old so we can tap into the new!

Today, I challenge you to step up and break out of your shell!

When a chick breaks out of its shell, it begins to experience life on a different level.

When we break out of old habits that hinder us from progressing and step into uncomfortable habits that stretch us, we begin to be fruitful and produce results that go beyond anything we can imagine.

God bless you and remember, JESUS LOVES YOU!

–52–

Today is a great day to rise above anything that weighs you down!

Today, let's choose to rise above anything and everything that tries to weigh us down.

We must choose to get up, no matter how deep we may think we have sunk. If we don't pick up our crosses, we might never see the light or even walk in our full purpose.

The devil will always bring distractions, but we don't have to remain distracted! Often, when we get distracted, we deviate and eventually quit! Let us not be quitters but pursue until the end.

The Bible tells us that greater is He that is in us (God in His full power) than he who is in the world (the devil, also known as the father of lies).

Let us not be intimidated! We are great, and therefore, we must expect great results no matter what! God surely is faithful!

God bless you and remember, JESUS LOVES YOU!

–53–

Today is a great day to serve God by serving those entrusted to you!

I believe God places specific people in our path for certain reasons and seasons.

Do not miss what God is doing in this season.

God often uses our acts of service to answer someone else's prayer. Your kindness today could be the encouragement that carries someone through their trial.

Some of you are those people that God placed in others' lives.

Let us remember that when we serve people whom God has entrusted to us, we are ultimately serving Him!

"Carry each other's burdens, and in this way you will fulfil the law of Christ."
Galatians 6:2 (NIV)

God bless you and remember, JESUS LOVES YOU!

–54–

Today is a great day to push through!

There are some places we will never get to unless we go through other paths. Are we willing to get uncomfortable and make difficult decisions temporarily so that we can enjoy a bountiful harvest at a later stage?

I continue to learn that in order to get TO, we have to go THROUGH! Let us not get stuck in or be discouraged by the "THROUGH" and keep our eyes focused on the "TO!"

I pray that you stay encouraged today to press forward!

God bless you and remember, JESUS LOVES YOU!

–55–

Today is a great day to trust God's leading!

We don't always have to wait for all the details to start. I know this goes against many beliefs.

I have come to learn that as we journey in this life with the Lord, He orders our steps! He directs and leads us to everlasting life. I believe where God leads, He feeds... where God guides, He provides. God's will is for God's bill.

Often, we have to take that first step in faith and trust in the leadership of Jesus through the Holy Spirit.

I'm reminded of a very popular scripture in Psalms 23:1 when the Psalmist wrote, "The Lord is my Shepherd, and I shall not want."

The Shepherd's primary concern is the sheep! God cannot lead us astray as His sheep!

Again, I say, where God leads, He feeds. Let's trust in His leadership today!

God bless you and remember, JESUS LOVES YOU!

–56–

Today is a great day to position yourself for a harvest!

Don't allow a season of waiting to discourage you from planting for the next harvest.

We reap because we sow, and we have to respect the seasons required for growth!

In the waiting, keep nourishing, watering, uprooting weeds, cultivating, and planting more seeds. Let's position ourselves for a harvest today!

God bless you and remember, JESUS LOVES YOU!

–57–

Today is a great day to identify your uniqueness!

You are not left behind!

Comparison will have you feeling as if you've been left behind. Do not fall for that!

God made each one of us unique and for a special and specific reason. You may feel as if you don't have much to give, but what scale is that based on?

Every part of you has value because all of you IS VALUABLE!!!

Tune into the voice of the Holy Spirit and ask God how He wants you to serve Him and others with your uniqueness.

God bless you and remember, JESUS LOVES YOU!

–58–

Today is a great day to worry less and trust God!

Learn to be present in every situation.

Sometimes we miss what's meant for a certain season
because we get caught up in the NEXT!

Lately, I have been learning to be present at every moment.
I believe that God orders our steps and that when we learn
to live in this truth, we will begin to see God's hand in
every part of our lives in a more personal way as our
Father.

I challenge you to worry less and trust God even more today!

God bless you and remember, JESUS LOVES YOU!

–59–

Today is a great day to speak life!

Sometimes we cease to become what we ought to be because of how we speak about ourselves.

The Bible tells us that life and death are in the power of the tongue, so whatever we say will either bring life or death over our lives!

If you are struggling to speak life over yourself, look at what God says to you, about you, and hold fast onto that!

ACTION

Find three scriptures that speak of how the Lord sees you or His promises for your life and meditate on them today.

God bless you and remember, JESUS LOVES YOU!

–60–

Today is a great day to yield!

Yield!!!

There's so much that God wants to do in and through us! I pray that we never hinder the move of God in our lives with our reasoning and limitations!

When God does something NEW, we need to be in a position to flow with what He is doing. When we say, "Use me Lord," we need to be prepared to be shaken outside of our norm!

Yield today!

God bless you and remember, JESUS LOVES YOU!

–61–

Today is a great day to be obedient!

Your obedience is the gateway to your breakthrough!

Isn't it funny how we often want the full details before we take that step of faith?

Sometimes God just wants a YES from us. Are you willing to say, "YES LORD," even when you are uncertain of the finer details?

ACTION

Let's take this time and listen to what God has entrusted to us in this season.

God bless you and remember, JESUS LOVES YOU!

–62–

Today is a great day to align with the Truth!

Some of you have believed a lie your entire life!

That lie can be, "I'll never be able to get out of this situation," or "I'm better off dead," or "I'll never change," or "I am a disappointment," or "nobody cares about me," or many of the other lies whispered to us.

Whatever contradicts what the word of God says about you is a LIE from the pit of HELL!!!

Do not fall for that trap! Listen. The word of God, also known as the BIBLE, is our mirror. We are what and who God says we are! Do not be deceived!

I pray that you break free from those lies today and align with the TRUTH!

God bless you and remember, JESUS LOVES YOU!

–63–

Today is a great day to steward what God has entrusted to you!

I always hear people say that the grass is greener on the other side...

I personally don't fully agree; if anything, I believe the grass is greener where you cultivate and water it!

You can't keep hopping from one thing to another while you have barely given your current assignment any of your time and effort!

Let us learn to steward well what God has entrusted to us!

ACTION

Take some time today to pick up assignments that you may have previously dropped. Find ways to move forward with what the Lord asked you to do.

God bless you and remember, JESUS LOVES YOU!

–63–

Today is a great day to harvest!

Life has different seasons, and I believe every season is essential for character building!

I decree and declare that you have entered your harvest season! Even in the harvesting, don't stop cultivating, sowing, nurturing, and watering in preparation for your next produce.

"For everything there is a season, and a time for every matter under heaven: a time to be born, and a time to

die; a time to plant, and a time to pluck up what is
planted."
Ecclesiastes 3:1-2 (ESV)

God bless you and remember, JESUS LOVES YOU!

–64–

Today is a great day to get rid of the old!

What are you willing to let go of to gain the "new" God has for you?

We've often heard and read that you can't expect to have new wine in an old wine skin.

I believe that this also refers to our mindsets. Unfortunately, some of our mindsets have been contaminated by previous experiences and circumstances. We must be intentional with getting rid of the old so that we can tap into the new. If it means starting to read a book, starving yourself of certain TV channels or streaming services or social media, tapping into new associations and many other uncomfortable adjustments, do that!

It is often difficult to dream of anything that we are not exposed to.

I challenge you today to be intentional!

God bless you and remember, JESUS LOVES YOU!

–65–

Today is a great day to reboot!

STOPOVERS ARE NECESSARY TO REBOOT, REFRESH, RECHARGE, THEN AFTERWARDS YOU CAN RESUME!

Sometimes we need to stop over and reboot!

Often, when my phone or any of my devices malfunction, I restart them, and that works every time!

Rebooting may not necessarily mean going away but simply unplugging yourself from anything that's draining you! You are allowed to do that!

It could be a negative environment or whatever that has ceased to yield fruit.

ACTION

Take a moment to assess as you step into this new day. What hinders you from rebooting?

God bless you and remember, JESUS LOVES YOU!

–66–

Today is a great day to pursue God's plan!

Sometimes we must bypass our plans to get to God's purpose!

Planning is good! Often, if we don't plan, we end up unproductive! But are we prepared to leave our plans to pursue God's intended purpose in our lives if God prompts us to do so? I pray that we become sensitive to God's voice that we know when we must pause our own plans, so we can see His purpose prevail!

God bless you and remember, JESUS LOVES YOU!

–67–

Today is a great day to be refined!

Our lives are in the hands of God, like a bow and arrow.

God is aiming at something you and I cannot see, and He continues to stretch and refine us. Even at times when we feel as if we can't stretch anymore or there's nothing else to give, God continues to refine us until the time has come for us to fly and soar like eagles.

Do you want to be stretched or remain stagnant? It is uncomfortable one way or another, but you have to choose your discomfort!

But who can endure the day of His coming?
And who can stand when He appears?
For He is like a refiner's fire
And like launderers' soap.
He will sit as a refiner and a purifier of silver;
He will purify the sons of Levi,
And purge them as gold and silver,
That they may offer to the Lord
An offering in righteousness.
– Malachi 3:2-3 (NKJV)

God bless you and remember, JESUS LOVES YOU!

-68-

Today is a great day to walk in VICTORY!

Elevation often attracts opposition.

As you tap into new and next levels, don't expect everyone to clap for you! Everyone means EVERYONE, including those that are closest to you!

Remember that our battles are not carnal but spiritual, so your rising might irritate some hidden demons. But!!! Do not despair; God fights for you!

Tap into this new day knowing that God has gone ahead of you, and you are walking in VICTORY!

DECLARATION

Thank You, Father, for accelerating me into new levels. Even as I ascend, I will not fear. I will not despair. I will walk boldly. I decree and declare that I am victorious in every area of my life.

God bless you and remember, JESUS LOVES YOU!

–69–

Today is a great day to choose to rise above!

Every day we have a choice, whether to get up or sleep – not only literally but also in all aspects.

We have a choice to rise above that which tries to pull us down. Daily!

The previous day, we looked at how elevation attracts opposition.

This portion reminded me of some characters in the Bible, especially David!

Many times, David had a choice to wake up or sleep, but he chose to rise above all that was sent to oppose him!

ACTION

Today, I want to challenge you to study more on the character of David in the Bible and write down some nuggets you glean from him.

God bless you and remember, JESUS LOVES YOU!

–70–

Today is a great day to stop doubting yourself!

STOP doubting yourself!

Often when we doubt ourselves, we find that we are on the right track.

That's it for today!

God bless you and remember, JESUS LOVES YOU!

–71–

Today is a great day to be disciplined!

When was the last time you disciplined yourself to do something that you didn't necessarily feel like doing, yet you knew very well you had to?

Well, today is that day! If we always wait to feel like doing something before we get started, we might wait for a very long time!

Discipline is doing what you committed to doing even when you don't feel like it at the present moment!

Discipline is what sets us apart!

Are you willing to be disciplined today?

God bless you and remember, JESUS LOVES YOU!

–72–

Today is a great day to take that step!

Take a step closer today! What promises are you holding on to?

Did you know that every day we are either moving forward, heading backwards or staying stagnant? We are faced with choices daily!

Today I want to challenge you to take a step closer – a small step is better than no step at all! You know what you need to do!

God bless you and remember, JESUS LOVES YOU!

–73–

Today is a great day to assess!

Today's word is ASSESS!!!

Every now and then, it is essential to take time out and assess! Taking time doesn't necessarily mean a holiday but can be a one-on-one with yourself to ask some uncomfortable questions.

I've realised that it's so easy to get carried away with everything happening around us that all we do is respond and react.

When we step back and assess, we place ourselves in a position to hear clearly from God.

Take some time to assess today. You may need to revisit some of your goals, dreams and even promises from God that you may have side-lined.

God bless you and remember, JESUS LOVES YOU!

–74–

Today is a great day to learn something new!

At one point in our lives, we have all had to do something for the first time, and there will always be something new to learn.

ACTION

Challenge yourself and look for something new to learn today!

God bless you and remember, JESUS LOVES YOU!

–75–

Today is a great day to be persistent!

You won't always feel like doing the things you NEED to do!

Have you ever noticed that it's often so difficult to do the things that you need to do? This can be praying, exercising, eating healthily, getting up earlier, working and many other things!

Why do you think it gets so difficult to do some of the things I just mentioned?

I believe it's because our flesh and mind are so resistant to change and discipline, but that is not an excuse for you not to execute.

Persist past resistance!

God bless you and remember, JESUS LOVES YOU!

–76–

Today is a great day to help someone!

I believe that we have overcome certain challenges, not so we can boast but to be a helping hand to those who are currently facing what we have conquered.

I believe God will send some people in your direction for this reason.

Today, I pray that we never miss what's on God's agenda. May we always be yielded so we can move in His seasonal timings.

God bless you and remember, JESUS LOVES YOU!

–77–

Today is a great day to keep believing!

"Ask and keep on asking and it will be given to you; seek and keep on seeking and you will find; knock and keep on knocking and the door will be opened to you."
Matthew 7:7 (AMP)

What are you trusting God for today? What have you been seeking? Have you been knocking?

I just wanted to encourage you with this word from the Bible spoken by Jesus Himself in **Matthew 7:7.**

Do not grow weary of doing good – even in your trusting season!

God bless you and remember, JESUS LOVES YOU!

–78–

Today is a great day to know your assignment!

We all have different assignments to fulfil, and every assignment has different requirements or resources. If we allow greed to stir envy and cause us to desire other people's resources, we might miss the assignment at hand!

Know your God-given assignment so that you can recognise the resources when God provides them!

God bless you and remember, JESUS LOVES YOU!

–79–

Today is a great day to praise!

Find a reason to praise today!

I know at times it may seem crazy to praise and give thanks to God, especially in the middle of some of the toughest situations.

One of my favourite characters in the Bible is King David, and one thing we can learn from him is that he praised and worshipped God in all seasons!

"Rejoice always."
1 Thessalonians 5:16 (ESV)

"Give thanks in all circumstances; for this is the will of God in Christ Jesus for you.
1 Thessalonians 5:18 (ESV)

God bless you and remember, JESUS LOVES YOU!

–80–

Today is a great day to get back up!

Not all setbacks are meant to set you back!

I am learning that even as we make our own plans, God's ways still prevail, and He always has our best interests at heart.

Sometimes we may think we are being set back, only to find that it's a divine detour or setup for a greater comeback. Now, I'm not saying that God is intentional about disappointing us; however, I am saying that let's aim to look for the good in all.

Some setbacks may be an opportunity for us to sharpen our tools and have our characters refined.

Don't allow yourself to stay down. Look for the lessons and rise. Get back up, child of God!

God bless you and remember, JESUS LOVES YOU!

Today is a great day to take action!

If we wait to feel like doing certain things, we might miss some important assignments!

At times you won't feel like doing important things, but that's when you must strengthen yourself in the Lord and pick yourself up.

Some assignments won't wait because we don't feel like taking action. Some of our assignments are time-bound.

I pray that your strength is renewed today as you trust in the Lord, so you may finish the race set before you well!

ACTION

Get a small notepad and start listing down top 5 things that you have been putting aside. As you complete them individually, rule them out or use a highlighter until you are done. Remember to set time or dates of completion for your own accountability!

God bless you and remember, JESUS LOVES YOU!

–82–

Today is a great day to run to God!

Stop being your own enemy!

Why do we often side with the devil? Why do we promote self-hate so much? No matter how "low" you may be feeling today, DO NOT COME INTO AGREEMENT WITH THE ENEMY'S LIES!

God does not hate you! Yes, you may currently be trapped in sin, remember God loves us but hates sin, which is why He sent Jesus Christ to die for the sin of mankind.

Run to Jesus today and repent! Listen to what He says to you and about you!

"For God so [greatly] loved and dearly prized the world, that He [even] gave His [One and] only begotten Son, so that whoever believes and trusts in Him [as Saviour] shall not perish but have eternal life."
John 3:16 (AMP)

God bless you and remember, JESUS LOVES YOU!

–83–

Today is a great day to stay focused!

Not everyone will understand your grind, and IT'S OKAY!

I know how lonely and discouraging it can get at times when you pursue what God has placed in your heart. Sometimes the only cheering we need is from the Lord Himself.

Stay focused!

God bless you and remember, JESUS LOVES YOU!

–84–

Today is a great day to receive God's mercy!

The mercy of the Lord is everlasting!

So many times, God gives us what we don't deserve instead of what we deserve. Because of God's mercy, we find ourselves overcoming that which was meant to drown us.

Today you have the opportunity to receive that mercy and grace as you step into a new day! Jesus Christ is at the door of your heart, knocking! Will you let Him and all of His mercy in?

PRAY

Lord, I thank You for Your mercies that are new every morning according to Lamentations 3:23. Holy Spirit, I ask that You keep me accountable so that I may fully be aware of God's mercies even in the smallest things. I thank You Father for Your goodness and mercy that follows me all the days of my life according to Psalm 23:6. In Jesus' Name. Amen.

God bless you and remember, JESUS LOVES YOU!

–85–

Today is a great day to make room for the NEW!

God will often give you more than you ever expected!

I love how God sets us up! God knows what we need for what He has called us to fulfil on this earth! Stop sidelining what the Lord is pouring out just because you are used to things being done a certain way!

It is time for the NEW! Make room for NEW!

"Do not remember the former things, Nor consider the things of old. Behold, I will do a new thing, Now

it shall spring forth; Shall you not know it? I will even make a road in the wilderness and rivers in the desert.
Isaiah 43:18-19 (NKJV)

God bless you and remember, JESUS LOVES YOU!

–86–

Today is a great day to have the Lord fill you up!

I believe that the Lord is pouring out new oil in this season.

We are living in the times that Jesus Christ foretold centuries ago. We need fresh oil and revelation so that we may be able to stand in this season!

Are you prepared for the Lord to fill you up?

PRAY

Father God, I ask You to fill me afresh. I thank You for the fresh oil that You are pouring upon me right now according to Psalm 92:10. Holy Spirit, I ask that You fill me afresh. Quench the thirst in my spirit. I yield completely to You. In Jesus' Name. Amen.

God bless you and remember, JESUS LOVES YOU!

–87–

Today is a great day to sow a good seed!

In a world where most people are hurt, choose to be the light!

What do I mean by that?

Today, you may be the reason why someone will change direction from planning to commit suicide to being joyous. Some people may look happy until you allow them a safe space to speak.

You may say, "Tshepy, I don't feel like it today. I don't have the energy; in fact, I am that person…"

I challenge you to pick up the phone, check on someone today and see how that will in turn help you too!

Sow a good seed today!

God bless you and remember, JESUS LOVES YOU!

–88–

Today is a great day to seek the face of Jesus!

While we continue to seek the blessing, let us remember to seek the Blesser!

I know sometimes we can get so consumed by our needs, but let's not forget to seek the face of Jesus in the midst of everything.

As we shift the focus from us to Him, we will begin to realise that ALL we need is in Him!

I am reminded of this scripture:

"For the [pagan] Gentiles eagerly seek all these things; [but do not worry,] for your heavenly Father knows that you need them. But first and most importantly, seek (aim at, strive after) His kingdom and His righteousness [His way of doing and being right – the attitude and character of God], and all these things will be given to you also."
Matthew 6: 32-33 (AMP)

God bless you and remember, JESUS LOVES YOU!

–89–

Today is a great day to wait!

One of the most crucial seasons in our lives is called
WAITING!

I know how frustrating waiting can be at times, especially
if "you've been waiting for so long".

Sometimes we'll never know how long we need to wait. Let
us not grow weary in the waiting season.

And as for [the rest of] you, believers, do not grow
tired or lose heart in doing good [but continue doing
what is right without weakening].
2 Thessalonians 3:13 (AMP)

Rejoice in the Lord!

PRAYER

Father , I know that You are faithful, even in the waiting season. I may not know how long I still have to wait, but I know that You are a Man of Your word. I believe that You are aligning everything for my good. In my waiting, I will meditate on your promises continually, knowing that You , Who promised, are faithful according to Hebrews 10:23. In Jesus' Name. Amen.

"My soul, wait silently for God alone, for my expectation is from Him."
Psalm 62:5 (NKJV)

God bless you and remember, JESUS LOVES YOU!

–90–

Today is a great day to exercise your power and authority!

Whatever you think you cannot achieve, you can!

God has given us so much power and authority.

Some of us may have been exposed to experiences that caused us to believe otherwise, but remember this truth: There is nothing you cannot do!

"I can do all things [which He has called me to do] through Him who strengthens and empowers me [to

fulfil His purpose—I am self-sufficient in Christ's sufficiency; I am ready for anything and equal to anything through Him who infuses me with inner strength and confident peace.]"
Philippians 4:13 (AMP)

Let this word be a reminder!

God bless you and remember, JESUS LOVES YOU!

–91–

Today is a great day – make the most of it!

A day wasted can never be relived. Make the best of today! Every single second, minute, hour, or day that passes can never be reclaimed!

It's almost as if we trade time for memories. What treasurable memories are you making in this minute?

How are you spending this hour that you will never get back? Let the Lord lead you into making the best of every part of today!

God bless you and remember, JESUS LOVES YOU!

–92–

Today is a great day to make room for God!

Are you willing to make room today and allow God to move freely?

Many of us are so used to God doing certain things in a specific way that when He does something new, we question it!

Remember, something new means something UNSEEN or UNHEARD of. It may take a while to adjust to it, but are you willing to try?

Be flexible in this season and see the Lord move mightily in you!

How can you get out of your own way today and allow God to be God?

God bless you and remember, JESUS LOVES YOU!

–92–

Today is a great day to sing a new song unto the Lord!

Don't wait for the platform when the Lord has already given you a song! Many of us stifle what God has placed in us just because other people fail to recognise it.

Not everyone will give you the platform to sing – sing anyway!

Those who are willing to listen will be drawn by your melody; all we do should be for the glory of the Lord!

God bless you and remember, JESUS LOVES YOU!

–93–

Today is a great day to recognise what's already in your hand!

God will always give you what you need for the season you are in.

Right now, you may feel as if you don't have any resources to execute your assignment, but listen… if you look carefully, you will see that you have what you NEED right now!

I hear the words, "What is in your hand?" – the same question that the Lord asked Moses!

Whatever you have right now may set you up for the generations to come!

PRAYER

Father God, just as you performed a miracle with what was in the hand of Moses, may you do the same for me.

Let my eyes be open to recognize a bountiful harvest that is concealed within the seed that is in my hand. In Jesus' Name. Amen.

God bless you and remember, JESUS LOVES YOU!

–94–

Today is a great day to equip yourself!

Pay attention to the equipping of the Lord in this season.

I believe we have entered a season where we need to get ready or rather stay ready because of what lies ahead. Equip yourself through praying and studying the word of God.

Do you make a point of spending time with the Lord daily in praying and studying the word? If not, start today. It will impact your whole life!!

God bless you and remember, JESUS LOVES YOU!

–95–

Today is a great day to rejoice!

Today is the day that the Lord has made! Let us rejoice and be glad in it!

So many wished to see this day but didn't. We did, and I believe the Lord Jesus still has a purpose that we all must fulfil.

Let us rejoice in this day!

God bless you and remember, JESUS LOVES YOU!

–96–

Today is a great day to be aware of the weight of your decisions!

Your life and everything about it, including the decisions you make daily, are not just about you.

I know society teaches us that we need to focus on ourselves, and it doesn't really matter who is happy or not with the decisions we make... BUT!!!...

"In the same way, let your light shine before others, so that they may see your good works and give glory to your Father who is in heaven." **Matthew 5:16 (ESV)**

This is a statement made by Jesus Christ Himself. If I were to try and summarise this, Jesus is saying:

"As a Christian – a born-again, spirit-filled believer in Christ – you are a light, so by default, you will attract, because that's what light does."

This means whether you care or not, someone is looking up to you. He continues to say, let people see YOUR GOOD WORKS, why? So that they may give glory to God, your Father in Heaven.

We always have to be mindful. We either draw people to Christ or push them away from Him through our deeds! We may be the only Bible someone reads, are we representing Jesus well as Christ followers?

God bless you and remember, JESUS LOVES YOU!

–97–

Today is a great day to stretch!

The very things you have been praying for will start to come alive before your eyes.

Do not push them away because you refuse to adapt.

Don't be surprised when your answered prayers begin to challenge YOU to stretch!

There is a shifting in the gears.

Get ready and stay ready!

God bless you and remember, JESUS LOVES YOU!

–98–

Today is a great day to be grateful wherever you are!

Some detours are necessary, for your benefit!

So many times, we plan things, and they don't often go as planned. Sometimes we may find ourselves in divine detours which are meant to stretch our faith in God. Are you prepared to trust God even when you can't see the path yet?

Today I challenge you to be grateful in every lane!

God bless you and remember, JESUS LOVES YOU!

–99–

Today is a great day to take the first step!

Sometimes all you need is to take the first step.

We often miss our destiny and divine moments because we want to see the complete puzzle. We will not need to use our faith if we already know what lies ahead. We will cease trusting in God and His ways if we only move when we see the next step.

Today I challenge you to take that step even when you don't know what lies ahead.

We may not know the next chapter, but we definitely know the Author!

God bless you and remember, JESUS LOVES YOU!

–100–

Today is a great day to hope in Jesus Christ!

There is hope on the other side of your trial!

Let us reflect on the crucifixion of Jesus Christ today... I cannot help but think of how the end of every season, births another.

You might be facing a moment that feels like the end — a time so dark that even the idea of hope seems out of reach. The thought of seeing light at the end of the tunnel may feel impossible.

But let me remind you of this truth: there is a light at the end of the tunnel.

I'm here to boldly declare that there is HOPE in Christ. No matter how deep the darkness, do not despair — for in Him, hope is alive.

Weep no more! The Bible tells us that weeping may endure through the night BUT joy comes in the morning! Hold on to that truth, knowing that we have overcome in and through Jesus Christ!

God bless you and remember, JESUS LOVES YOU!

–101–

Today is a great day to trust God's timing!

Not every delay means that you are on the wrong path.

Sometimes we find ourselves faced with a temptation to abort the mission just because we are faced with a minor delay. Some delays are an opportunity for us to gear up and get ready for the road ahead. Other delays may be for our own protection.

We need to always hold dear to the truth and reality that God's promises are YES and AMEN!

God bless you and remember, JESUS LOVES YOU!

–102–

Today is a great day to let go and let God!

Some situations will require you to step out so that you may witness the full manifestation of God's glory.

I know most of us are so used to being involved in everything to a point where "letting go and letting God" gets uncomfortable... or am I the only one?

There comes a point where certain things can only move without our hands being involved. Are you willing to surrender to God today and this week? Are you willing to let go and completely let God?

God bless you and remember, JESUS LOVES YOU!

–103–

Today is a great day to execute your assignment!

Some assignments are assigned only to you.

It is okay to delegate but remember that there's a level of grace and anointing that rests on you for this task at hand!

God bless you and remember, JESUS LOVES YOU!

–104–

Today is a great day to glorify God with your uniqueness!

There are certain things that only you can do, the way only you can!

Sometimes we write ourselves off because of past failures and criticism from those who failed to identify our unique purpose and calling.

Why write yourself off when God has called you to be uniquely you?

I've said this before, and I'll say it again, find what God has placed in you and use it to glorify Him. As we become less, He becomes greater in us.

God bless you and remember, JESUS LOVES YOU!

–105–

Today is a great day to obey the Holy Spirit!

I've come to realise that one step of obedience could hold the key to another door.

The mystery about this life we live is that we will never know what lies on the other path. Unfortunately, we can't decide on one thing without forsaking the other. Does this make sense? Every time we take a step forward, we leave one chapter and step into another.

Personally, I am grateful for the grace and mercy of our Lord. I am grateful for the Holy Spirit, who is our Helper.

We know that we can yield and lean on Him as we progress on this earth.

SAY THIS

Holy Spirit, I submit myself to Your leading today. I empty myself before You. Fill me up. Lead and use me as You will. In Jesus' Name. Amen

God bless you and remember, JESUS LOVES YOU!

–106–

Today is a great day to soak in His faithfulness!

Step out today knowing that God has already gone ahead of you.

"You go before me and follow me. You place your hand of blessing on my head."
Psalm 139:5 (NLT)

I know sometimes the road may look rocky, but remember Jesus Christ is your Solid Rock and HE IS FAITHFUL IN EVERY SEASON!

I encourage you today to dive into the Word of God – The Holy Bible and see God's promises to you. Soak in His faithfulness and watch your faith arise.

God bless you and remember, JESUS LOVES YOU!

–107–

Today is a great day to be rooted in Christ!

You will never find a tree begging for fruit to sprout from it. Why? Because the tree is planted, and it was created to produce when planted!

Where are you planted? What fruit are you producing? I am not saying you are a tree; however, the Word of God in **Matthew 7:20** says we will know people by their fruit.

The beautiful thing about not being a tree is that you can move.

If you don't like the fruit, check the roots!

Be planted in Jesus Christ today. He is the Way, the Truth, and the Life!

In **John 15**, Jesus said that if we abide in Him and He, together with His Word, abide in us, we will bear fruit.

God bless you and remember, JESUS LOVES YOU!

–108–

Today is a great day to be a vessel!

The other day I was having a conversation with my son, and I remember saying something like ...

"It's not about the masses. It's about the impact."

I had to pause and write that down. Isn't it funny how masses and crowds are usually associated with success? No, I am not discrediting numbers. If anything, it is true that numbers don't lie. In this case, one is a number too!

I challenge you today to look for one person and be a blessing to them. It does not necessarily mean financially, but also through acts of kindness or service. Any way that you can! Do it!

Be a vessel today!

God bless you and remember, JESUS LOVES YOU!

–109–

Today is a great day to finish STRONG!

You have everything you need to complete the assignment.

The word assignment has been so strong in my spirit. I believe that we have entered a season where most of us must carry what we laid aside for so long and finish strong!

READ AND MEDITATE ON PHILIPPIANS 1:6 TODAY

I am convinced and confident of this very thing, that He who has begun a good work in you will [continue to] perfect and complete it until the day of Christ Jesus [the time of His return].
Philippians 1:6 (AMP)

All those responsibilities you have been skipping and walking around – this is the picking-up season. The grace is sufficient to carry you through. Are you willing?

God bless you and remember, JESUS LOVES YOU!

THANK YOU!

PRAISE THE LORD!

"I will praise the Lord with my whole heart, in the assembly of the upright and in the congregation."
Psalm 111:1 (NKJV)

Thank you for allowing me to spend the past few days with you!

Although this may seem like the end, it is not it!

I pray that this devotional stirred you to have dominion over your day. Moreover, that you have grown in your walk with the Lord and experienced a great transformation from the inside out. Our greatest desire should be to grow deeper in our intimacy with Jesus Christ and be more like Him.

My prayer is that you will make a decision to step into the life that God has called you to and abandon every lie that has attached itself to you and your bloodline. I pray that you will step up and be the one that your future generation will thank. May you break every barrier and soar in and through Christ Jesus.

I would like to give you an opportunity to make Jesus Christ your Lord and Saviour if you have not done so already and make heaven your eternal home. The bible tells us in **Romans 10:10** that "For with the heart man believeth unto righteousness; and with the mouth confession is made unto salvation." So let's pray together:

Heavenly Father, I thank You for sending Your Son Jesus Christ to die for me. I believe that Jesus Christ is the Son of God and that He died on a cross, rose on the third day and will return to earth for me. I receive this gift of salvation; I forgive everyone who has hurt or offended me, and I receive Your forgiveness. Father. I confess that Jesus is my Lord and Saviour, and I will live for Him from this day on until I see Him face to face. Thank You Father. In Jesus' Name, Amen.

If you prayed this prayer, either for the first time or multiple times, I would like to personally congratulate you and say welcome to the family of God.

If you are reading these very words, I would like to congratulate you once again for finishing what you started!

Please feel free to connect with me and share how you have experienced this devotion on info@tshepym.co.za. I would love to hear from you!

One last time: God bless you and remember, JESUS LOVES YOU!